In the Absent Everyday

In the Absent Everyday

—

Tsering Wangmo Dhompa

Tsering Wangmo Dhompa
2017

Apogee Press
Berkeley · California
2005

For Ama,
of course.

Acknowledgements

I'd like to thank Elaine Seiler and Melvin Shaffer who sent me to school. To Dickey Wangmo, Dechen Tsering, Marilyn Kennell, Marilyn Seaton, Mausumi D, Norbu Tenzing, & Valerie Melvin—thank you. Kabir Mansingh Heimsath for the cover photo. Dan Featherston who accepted In *Writing The Names* for A.bacus before it became *Rules of the House*.

My gratitude to the following people and publications where the following poems have appeared:

Sylvester Pollett for BACKWOODS BROADSIDES featuring
    A matter not of order
Bob Arnold of Longhouse Press for a booklet featuring the poem,
    In the absent everyday
Andrew Schelling, Editor of *Picking Up Stones: 28 Poets of Buddhist
    North America* (2005) for Autonomy of the mind.
BIRD DOG: Just the tools, Two years of winter
BOSTON REVIEW: By the wayside
CALL: Formal Links and Surrender (formerly Constitutional)
CRAYON: 4, He names, Striped damsel, Altar, (formerly untitled)
    Life of dust and mangoes (formerly untitled), Apology (formerly
    untitled)
HINGE: A BOAS ANTHOLOGY: Intention, Error, Review, Explosion of
    tires has no meaning, Life of roses (formerly from Irrevocably so)
MAGAZINE CYPRESS: Things to Remember, On 21st Street, Silver and
    Game
POETRY SALZBURG: Game, Things to remember
TWENTY SIX: Construction of his taste, Dry beds in the sun
RANGE: Life of roses and Tonic ruse
SKANKY POSSUM: Introduction
TUNDRA: An ending to a love story (formerly Endings), After the night,
    Spotless pots
-VeRT: City of Tin (www.litvert.com)
XANTIPPE: To my friend who works

Book design by Philip Krayna Design, Berkeley, California.

ISBN 0-974468770. Library of Congress Catalog Card Number 2004117968.

Published by Apogee Press, Post Office Box 8177, Berkeley CA, 94707-8177.
www.apogeepress.com

Table of Contents

A matter not of order

ONE

You eat with your right hand.
Prop the broom away
from your body. Strike.
A roof of wool, a bed of skin.
A follicle for food. A hand of error
and infliction is given to all.
The left hand heeds
prayer beads. The left hand
signals retreat.
What is your good name?
Where are you from?

TWO

I was taught not to ask for more.
I took the smallest pieces,
left the last on the plate to deities,
bullies and elders. Train eyes,
the elders said, to want
what is already yours. So I stayed
out in the woods till jackals howled
and picked from the streets what was
lost or cast off. Sang songs
to a kindergarten teacher
who wore pink checkered dresses
and spoke in English when cross.
Now bigger is a sign of competence.
Was my heart stitched for this?
I am drifting into a world of enquiry
to quantify, qualify, even as
around me, summer performs.
Beetles, coal stunned in sun.
And little birds in gray
sing madly for food or love.

THREE

You are placated
with offerings
hollow as midnight's ankles.
Day life postpones impulses
to the *future* as though it sits
ahead with a symbol for permanence.
In night life you dream
a daughter. Skin a beast.
You can tell you are good.

FOUR

Bottles you save
because they can still hold
something of use. Two,
three gimcracks allowed.
The window sill incumbent
with the regret of envy.
Come in. Come in, said the
obedient citizen to the witch.
Come in. Come in. Entries
of flowers in bloom.

FIVE

I know you by your walk
because we are from the same country.
If you were here to give safe passage—mosquitoes,
daddy-long legs, mollusks underwater—would
be left to their job. West surrenders
to a new language. Bellwether.
Billingsgate. Bivouac. Let us go
south. Let us go east. We come to be
courted. Or hands emptied.

SIX

Conquered by ingredients: we replace salt
with sugar. Butter with milk.
We believe others know better
because we've arrived to find our place taken.
Your hands blunt from obeying.
Your name is happy days
and wisdom. What cannot be explained
is accepted. Our forefathers went
to bed with salted butter tea in their bones.
You are living the life given.
You drink sweetened tea at three
in the afternoon. Adjust cup to saucer.
Your gullet adhering to silence.

SEVEN

The first drop of blood
appeals to a past. We learn
to love the land of our
fathers and mothers because
we love them.
Walk on your forehead.
Where you are
is who you are.

EIGHT
for Monica Dengo

Once in the year of the iron horse, the river
changed course and your house was built.
I am the foolish one seeking old treasures
when monkeys still steal from our verandahs.
When we say rock, shell, sand, labor is not
intended. Rocks selected for you.
The lines in my palm follow weather predictions,
stock predictions, thinking experts must be heeded.
Must consistency be an illusion? Here, pick up
dandelions, watch seeds bellow into air.
Wish to desire. It's the human way.

NINE

The appearance of a crow
throws the morning into distemper.
Children's haircuts are postponed.
New plans are made after referring
to numerical charts and the whereabouts
of the mad dog last seen chewing a shoe
at the gate. The elders remember events
related to a crow's previous entry. It's not
just the coming winter. Fire crackers go off
in the neighbourhood. Someone is preparing
her nuptial bed; a room of newly acquired
tokens. Dogs keep their normal routine.
Everything is partially revealed.

TEN

How simple it would be
and to our best interest
to offer what we have to bandits.
We have climbed the mountain
passes, offered prayers and ruminated
on the possibility of tumbling over
the edge. Many hours of rain and the road
is a river. Grasslands bronze as nomads
move closer to their winter holes.
This world is a lie. I think of all
the futures you will miss. Life goes
by the center. We are drinking.
We are eating.

In the absent everyday

Again, it is colour I remember.
Not octagonal, not collapsing inwards
like defeated butter, the way father said
we wouldn't, if we truly were boys.
I am always receiving messages from people
I haven't met. The understatement of her
heel. The smells we could not name
without comparing. But for comparisons,
would love be here. The wind bends trees
like cotton puppets while inside this room
nothing moves without being lifted.
The revolution of a seed in air.
We have let our dialect avoid our throat,
there are no flying men. Think of
the opposite, says the wise one. The way
the ancients from the East did. Now
all of a sudden, tradition is good.
Ink was blue when I learned to write.

All day it rained. The hills huddled
like teenage girls in their first ankle length dresses.
Clothes meant for washing disappeared
into corners. The princess stayed in her tower,
as is best, given the regimen of the clouds.
All day—daffodils—through perforated curtains.
I am no longer of use, my breasts too full.
Chilli tongue. I cannot name the capital
of countries with the lowest mortality rates.
Ants and insects scurry to stay dry. I see
where they could go but do not lead them.
Nothing is said. New shoots push
against feet. All hushed for a green anxiety.

Fern moss covers a name on the wall
and so a story becomes secret. Someone
we know dresses in the dark and wishes
to see texture or smell. Silver prickly?
Someone is blessed with a long-life initiation
as a recently orphaned grasshopper leaps
to attach herself to a growing tree.
The visible through finicky and furrowed
territories. Oh heart, coward. Step out.
Step out. White underclothes flap towards
the cries of the sick woman who names
the dead in her room as she flees from
a tightly woven sleep. Her hair knotted
into a barnacle. She begs for her mother.
Pigeons keep a distance, then wrangle
over worms edging backwards into the earth.

Your third eye has given up sight.
Summer has made an excuse of this
distance we keep. There is war
in the vicinity. Too long on my own.
(I have reflected.) Ought I
to have lied more? Am I sorrier
than I know to be? In my dreams
as a little girl, a man is swept away
by a tall feather. I watch. I wait.
I do not arm to rescue
with my plastic knitting needles
and cooking knives of paper.

We are on vacation but no closer
to learning terms for the familiar.
A village barks into night.
The hills with their wild flowers
orchestrate a drama, then headaches.
We're dizzy with the riot of colours
we have sometimes worn. Violets again,
embedded into the ground. Violets
chosen for storytelling and pliant.
And here, this palm of many heartaches,
studying, steadying for a purpose.

The idea of a decision is a decision.
We build arguments around impermanence
but are not the sort of people to admit
to inconstancies. Keeping the almanac
of the day in mind, the lover whispers
to his love. If parents are happy, if the red robed
one predicts harvest, yes, then it is indeed fate.
The word sorry said too often brings the
clothesline down. Women understand
(such indirect ways) we learn to say.

The mountains refuse trees,
spit flowers scarlet and lavender.
The only ocean here is rain. From
no image comes an understanding
how the life we have lived does not go
away with wishing. Wishing, this hour
past midnight. How romance overtakes
all sentinels of sense. Somewhere,
a man slips into stolen socks. The
tautness of unstretched cotton leads
him to believe the day will be fulsome.
This is not what he learnt in school.
Flowers plead under a billion feet.
Another day dissolves to flies
foraging inside radish leaves.

Hollyhocks plot with the sidewalk
to befuddle the expected. The legitimacy
of one lie does not absolve you.
In my reasonable life desire is
an inevitable concurrence. Researchers
want to know how I get my news
and do I like it. I do not read
the newspaper so benevolent industry
would be happy to send me a free
subscription. You will pay nothing
a voice says on the phone. People will
be killed every day, new stars will
be named. On this planet, the sun
will follow its route and shun a proposal
to delay. Days, taciturn as a tattoo tucked
under a shirt, slip unseen, away.

The mountain air must see
time as passing in present.
The elders say times have
changed, as though they'd
forego a year if it was up
to them. Days grow in them
like a potato. They see
their body as a map
to the country's center
from where the young
never return the same.
Nothing is spectacular,
without a reference. Or
does that change? Snow
traps everything for a while.
The river stops flowing. ·

It was said that dancing in a parking lot
was not an auspicious beginning. Henceforth,
the elders said, love would be fickle.
It is always the elders who have the last word.
There will be other and better venues
to plan the perfect future. You understand
how it all works. That distance has a nerve
where it recoils. That rock is meant for
pleasure is permissible. In the old days,
women could not say no. In the old days,
women would not say yes. The mountain
you wish to climb will always be there.

Home, we say, whenever we are afraid
of what we see around us. When we were
young we had wishes postponed to the future
because we could not choose. When we
were young, you say, we completed
a living. Sentences shaped like the swallow
of your throat. When the pied piper comes
to this town, you will hide your shoes
and cover your ears. The river will not rush,
the mountains will not cleave. Chocolate
trees will bend so you can lick
their sweat off. It will all end happily, again.

City of tin

Politeness prohibits saying what I really think.
Viaduct: a code for a feeling. Like mauve
over the street of tarmac, a grave summer day
offering painted toe nails and a leg longer by perspiration.
Or gannets in sight. That women are said to speak so much
of feelings, as though to clarify would mean the end.
It never is. Clarification I mean. To indicate trust
I tell you the fish is who I look at most these days.
For love, for love. Endings happen. Words I use
because I like who I become. Give me nothing. Tiny,
tiny pebbles used as prop. Tilted and tinted glass.
City of my desire has lines rigged at the waist.
One minute of sleep at a desk might bring
it all down. Words you find under my nail.
(S)wallow. Some night owl effusion.

Intention

Spring, across this border. Talk of green of trees and layers of morning. Still, this question about how we really feel as night slips on like a fisherman's hand in sea weed. The necessity to link the heart to things that matter. Mother's dance to *Jungle Boy,* her breast freed from rhythm. Petunias for sale in a hardware store. Pistons and objects made for strong arms. Or streets where half open doors reveal women in heels that indicate, among the obvious, this desire to reach. You know everything ought to be forgiven. The existence of objects, that they should also be. Cracks on the marble waylaid by winter's apathy sucumb to mishaps. An irenic pact suggesting entry; inter; yes sir, yes madam, please enter.

Error

You wish to be presented formally, preferably by a relative
who has merely heard of you. Accept it to be equivocal.
Two mentions of your adversity to flowers. I could point
towards a childhood and you'd be clear of all blame.
Not far from a view of your city, mimosa in frugal yellow
wraps the edges of a driveway. I am writing around you.
You have entered this kingdom. Give a little hope.

Altar

The coming of brigands into this area of ordered civility.
Still, politeness could be applied. We say *please, oh, please.*
What we mean is, we are alone. Please remember she can
be of practical help. Her hands, long and lean. Fishermen
want her. Thieves keep what they take but for a price
they exchange. A single passport must prove the
sovereignty of my country. How gold was
claimed in this land. How a monkey and a woman beget
a people. Her braid in local tongue. We take these to
show we were a nation. This is now a history lesson.

Review

Part of the confusion lay in the way light appeared on the
horizon like a thin sheet of marmalade. You were not
prepared for it. You were not talking about life but that was
present too. There's a movie about a day-dreaming mechanic
whose car stays in the passing present. Letters from dissident
friends, and the birth of four reincarnate lamas in our little
town. Soon, your fate will be proclaimed. Summer like
a rash. Letters again, but still, who can say where one finds
resolution. Fingers without guile, soft as a kitten's throat.
Fire flies around. You are already there.

Explosion of tires has no meaning

In an attempt to speak of you, I have thrice resorted
to achromatic gestures. Granted we have not had time
to discuss the growth of intimate beings. Flowers around
were hiding. Dogs chewed into their barks. The prince
declared his love for a common girl and the parliament
dissolved before astrologers could be reached. If I send
you love letters it is because this is not the age for it.
Fugitive and fulcrum. Our nights sighing away from us.

Apology

Wherein we matter, words raising evaporable walls
and conduit vaporous or vapid. A plain field is
canter-friendly and food. How is it that we come to dreaming
without purpose. Think, the more we know, the less we become
capable of dreaming. If only I had fealty to speak of. If only
cormorants would come closer where we are cutting up words.
Happy. You are my volant being. *Happy, happy.* A wing is voyage.
An artery is to reconsider. Matter is to disintegrate.

Malady for groove

You are not taught to see too far into the future.
You have secrets for a reason. The betrayal
of identity, cumin in pores. The yellow of turmeric
lingering for days under nails. This world is spinning,
rain is rain, and again, we are surprised that soldiers die.
The measure of fulfillment is to know there is no more
out there than was. I have not forgotten what my mother
was to me, still, there are days when I have nothing new.
Not enough to say this is why. Yet a heart beats. All the
possibilities of a syncretic solution from experience
and illusion make for a consistency that involves
strangers and deadlines: a weatherman, a garbage
collector, the Friday morning special on flowers.
No memory for folly. Yet a heart beats.

Life of bows

The plan is to keep contained within easily defined needs.
The forms we aspire to. The bow as a source
of accomplishment (if you are a hunter). The bow
on a wall, without a specific task is malleable content.
A singular sigh may yet uproot all. But here we are
stacking sentences like a nervous habit. Now rising,
now sinking within the cordiality of our defenses.
The indentations of tongue made and then given
to lose in such and such a pursuit. But ah, memory
to secure at will. And poetry before the hour of silence.
Your aperçu making trees grow taller. Actor and spectator.

Life of roses

Do not bring red roses. I do not like them. This tirade of
summer asphalt. (Perhaps here is another lesson that one
heartache is too little for this life). Apology of dry lips while
winter days are put to the test and measured in cups of tea.
Then again, the linearity of thought is just an abstraction.
Decisions made against letters yet to be opened while hair
for ornament and hair for ambush become a stalemate.
All around atoms are forming. Remembrance alone is static.
The earth shifts under and we are rooted on pillar legs.
We are wading into the shallow pools of water. We are
writing to say we are kind and we are here. We are alone
and time is still time.

He names

He wishes for the whole to be revealed at once.
How when lost, the structures surrounding are familiar
but hidden as though he is dreaming the streets
he is on. He wants the sinking feeling of not knowing
how far home is. He has names for those whose absence
troubles him and methods to measure pain. Every new loss
calling on the old over and over should genealogy comfort.
That sorrow is present does not surprise him. He doubts
experience strengthens him. He contemplates taking new vows.
Of telling his mother she was wrong: that fate is a fool.
In his dreams he has never screamed. He is not the hero
but diction is on his side. There is no corner beyond reach
yet he leaves them to cobwebs. This is his life, he thinks.
He names each spider. Says hello, hello gentlemen and ladies.

Waiting for Marcos

Tiny, tiny marks carved from her.
Dogs on their haunches
like cloches framing
a head. Something so perfect
she says. First came the fear
of the unknown. This life
of supple desires—having come here,
it suffices. Suffuses. Fingers digited
for looping. How wide is the day,
she thinks. Then records the ailing
relatives. The rabbit in the sink.
The half-full room beside hers.
A whirl has arrived at the door.
Windows that lead to water
and void. Wide. And longer than all
rivers strung together.

An ending to a love story

Prior to undertakings, let the parameters be known.
If you are uncertain, do not give hope. Blind horses
carry her to a gate. Adamant heart, she says to herself
in the middle of a crowded bus. No one suggests she tell
her story. A bridge ties his city to hers. Her childhood toy
of pink wool lies under her grandma's bed. In the end,
she tells herself, nothing is sustainable. Battles have been
fought over insects. The mayor takes hours in hand,
declares the city can afford to have one more day as holiday.
For someone dead, as is customary. She decides her happiness
must be taken into account; even in this situation, certainly
in such a situation. She cuts an apple in three equal parts.
Carves her favorite word into its snow flesh.

Dry beds in the sun

Certain facts hadn't been accounted for—sons have killed for less than money. Long hours by the bed while listeners mourn for the way life accepts its route. Karma, it is said, allows no change. Legends of the town made the place seem larger. We took it on foot and late at night, shared air not covered with insects. It was summer and moths clung to the floor in the morning like drunk kids asleep on park benches. Four people died in the neighborhood; it was said that three of them had cases of the liver. That disease should take them was a relief to their bodies pushed to live by relatives. They said they were like trucks abandoned in the high passes. What other option had we, with nothing but the ordinary. After more prayers, the butter lamp enacted its last drop and the elders said it was time to sleep. You get used to everything, they said, as though solicited for an answer. The mourning lasted for forty-nine days. Mothers took longer. Said it was their way.

Striped damsel

In a village not far from her town, a cow gave birth
to a calf with two heads. Black and white they were.
For days people came to visit the cows insisting on a miracle.
The story made her reflect she was in the wrong place.
She wondered if her understanding of the world grew narrower
with age, if good eyesight replaced wisdom. She would like to
clean the windows but there is a storm coming into town. Then
what? Her eyelashes are losing root. Her toe bulbous and
broad. She wants to be happy but feels hurried or conspired
against. She cannot remember the names of invertebrates. She
would like to know her plants. The garden she will have. The
life she will live. Later.

Life of suffering

Daffodils are thrusting out of dampness. Particulars are
listed: cherry blossoms in the square, sartorial practicality
releasing calves whiter than the beach. His purple nails.
Sipping tea, looking out the window while birds are with
their kind, all chattery. Where is the fear? The affability
of spring supposes everything is new and stationary.
We know it takes fear, not faith to believe all that we see.
Tertiary colours become you. Consider lotus legs, loaves
of bread, or wine as an exercise towards an uncomplicated
happiness. Everything loses its function when broken down.
You of the dead, you I love more than anyone. Consider.

The construction of his taste

He is livid behind his mask in the photo. Later, he wonders
if that did him any good. The object of his anger
reads out a passage to him and he hears *flotsam*. He thinks
mendicant because flotsam can be a vagrant.
He worries he is living through associations, that too many
choices are given to live out life. She is his sister and does
not know him. What is it about flesh and blood that makes us
so foolish? Nothing, yet he would kill for her happiness.
Blind children are painting in the yard behind him. They know
the boundaries of the paper. They paint without desire to see
what is created but can tell you what they have memorized.
Perhaps that is all one needs to know, he thinks. He writes
in the center of his palm, *taxonomy of my dislike:* he can
taste it. Coffee ought to be only black, he thinks.

By the wayside

Mrs. Dondup says life is not a happy lollipop
and she has said that before. Not in so many words
but when her brother lost his house in a neighbourhood fire,
and she went out to save what she could while he drank
himself to sleep—she said she was—washing her hands
of his affairs. Then next morning was seen cleaning
the yard of embers. She is sitting with mother ·
who upon losing her composure is crying into her hands,
Really, I would understand everything, if he would only...
Somehow I always lose her last words. They sit before
the window; how still the world is beyond mother's shaking
shoulders and Mrs. Dhondup running back and forth
between tea on the stove and cleaning rags, which she puts
against mother's cheeks. She taps her finger against the window
to dislodge the ant walking on the outside. She points towards it
and it becomes the object of their compassion. Mother looks
at the ant, and beyond to endless minutes, anticipating a lesson.
Life is not a happy lollipop, she says. Her fingers reach
for the window as though to wipe away the image before her.
It is her own but she is looking at something else.

Tonic ruse

He carries symbols in his head. They are
forms; they are light, not willed nor bought.
And he as tenant, arranges them
as though they were mangoes. Feeling for maturity
in epidermia, for the curvature of ear and eye as he would
at the morning market. He thinks of a one time love,
whose willow lashes dragged to her cheeks. He does not know
what he wants from her. Or from the lover, she who ran
faster with heels. His images too are singular. Midnight
on his hips, dazzles the mirror. No one who sees this
can say he is not perfect. That rivers don't rush
towards the moon. That the sunless night is a dark
and quiet aphid over sleeping travelers. Wading. Waiting.

Life of dust and mangoes

On rainy days she takes her feet into consideration,
gathers all the creases in her face into a knitted
handkerchief. The feared comes again and again,
never placed or given its time. In the history of
a family are some rarely understood because they have
everything expected in them. They say she is ordinarily
common. She can hear birds before anyone else and
knows their habits. Children want her stutter and her
orange sandals. They would like her to be their imaginary
friend called Volkin or Tatrani. She knows she must not
plan towards anything because there is nothing sworn
to her. Knows the earth is no kind benefactor waiting
with blue blossoms in hand. Only once she was mistaken
thinking that trees grew from her uncle's spittle.
When he died while resting under a mango tree
in mid-spring she reckoned he was not a person to rely on.
After he died, the walls around his house seduced
all the dragonflies in the neighbourhood. Such an
account is verifiable but serves no purpose.

A character whose name I forget

This question of desire or its equivalent erupting
from caudal concerns. How a man walked all night
in black hush to discover hunger and loneliness
in fields of heliotrope, and the stars, belonging to the night,
not his. Never his. He is from a book so I relate to him.
I am unable to interpret the function of a heart while
the body must be fed through purchases and contracts.
Reading suffering in phrases; thinking this is how others live.
No one is there to say otherwise. In the story, the man
never recovers from the walk. Keeps his eye attentive to the path,
till he is killed ironically, by accident. And then of course,
it does not matter. To remember this man from all
stories heard makes him sadder. Still, it does not matter.

Spotless pots

Nothing in her life, she liked to say, prepared her for this.
They were never sure what she was referring to. When she
said *this,* her fingers pointed towards a metal spoon
embedded in the wall. A remnant of a passionate outburst.
It was uncertain if she was party to it. Another time her gaze fell
on her child. Immediately, he said he always knew he was loved
less than intended. He wanted to say he wasn't loved enough.
When these uprisings came, she'd say she had sweated
two T-shirts full. Her language allowed for no misinterpretations.
A country is a funny place she'd say, you begin to think one person
will not be affected by terms like *gross national product,* but he is.
She ate from banana leaves and stainless steel. Nothing leaking,
she would say. Nothing lost. They looked for signs to disinter
her needs. She was a yearling. They saw she liked yellow flowers
in winter, talcum powder, and an occasional local whiskey.

Mimi's poem

This then must be the only recourse,
the benefit of hands within contours.
There were days when the evening light entered the room
with surprising meekness. Her surly lines palmate on the floor,
the chair thrown out of its usefulness. And the height of the hour;
not appropriate for any ritual—time as waiting or vacant.
Again, I am throwing all senses into sense. Why must we seek
perfection at all? Heart things are applicable everywhere.
There is a little dog and she is far away. In the past, a statute
of love meant whet, meant whirl—apposition of self.

Your eyes of silver.
Your lips of mulberry.

After the night

As light evades her room she is afraid shadows will reveal
indignities she has escaped. That sorcerers will lift their skirts
and send thoughts to stick to her like damp leaves. She gathers
her belongings before sleep, thinking this will be the night to
explain mysteries of the past. It is rarely fear we leave behind
in childhood. A paper holds her name and address, just in case;
this she puts near her pillow night after night. The fear
of the resolute, like armies marching into a blind night singing
love songs. She wonders if protection comes from prayers.
In the morning she laughs, calls herself a silly thing and the
night is forgotten. Or accepted as an advantage. Far away in
the future of her tongue are promises of condiments.
Turmeric. Saffron. Nights irresponsible as statues in the
bazaar. These are pledged. Surely we can live again and again
the same lesson. In her dream comes a mother who has lost
her street address. She speaks no English and holds a key.

Introduction

He comes to mind as a city. How the body of the ground
fits the curvature of the eye and a decision is made to see it
as a field of cauliflower or the belly of a watch. In any case,
the first association made is made. He is a lone sailor rowing
to where ducks teach ducks to fish. Pema Karpo. Now Agnes
Drum falls behind her chicks. One step a day he thinks will take
him closer to the end. And the one with gray stripes penciled
across her head, yet unnamed, has taught herself to flip onto
her stomach. He peers into the water, decides her name must
be monosyllabic and fire.

Glass of orange

She begins to write to a man she has never met. She does not
know if he exists but feels the imminence of belonging.
Perhaps his fingers are plucking pieces of glass beads
narrower than a blink. She is not prepared for the way he will
look but wishes him to be entirely other than her expectations
of how a man should be. She thinks of wild yellow poppies
holding tight on open hills where winds come with rude
tongues to pluck them. A man is surrounded by beads small
as carraway seeds. He is building a necklace for the woman he
loves most. He ruminates in a way that makes her more than
a lover and less than a mother. She begins to think this
explains the whole of her. When she conjures the man she
wants to love, she thinks of characters in comic books.
She is unable to make up her mind: is alarmed it has
something to do with timidity. Or intellect. She likes
afternoons best when it is still possible to begin new thoughts.
There is a fisherman. There is a fisherman spreading his net
into water, locking air into his lungs, then giving it all up. Fish
swim to him. He watches them squirm. Drops them in.

Jim's running across the bridge

In these hours hunched into our day
we say what is acceptable. We are hidden
from the sun but there's a full day of living
still left. You know how a warm wind turns
arms into wings so that the ground under
unravels as it travels. In the commonplace
rituals of a day we don't see tubers that are
pushing tiny horns soon to grow into a little
girl's favorite bower. Flowers will bloom.
The right lane will close for emergency repairs
and big sales will coincide with major holidays.
The questions you mean to ask are already
irrelevant. It's that simple after all.

Betty goes downtown

In any given situation the illusion of an alternative comes later.
Opening avenues suddenly as though prudence and wisdom
were always there to be consulted. Or experience, if relevant.
But here again Betty, the family fish, bangs into her reflection
all day. She is forgetful we say. Perhaps she likes herself too much.
And this is our love, sending our sons and daughters to war
so they can learn to serve this country, president, car.
Someone we know is always falling in love with a charlatan.
He is happy, he is happy, he says. We say rogues know happiness
or how to present it. What does it matter in the end?
In the end is not a place. In the end is the curl in the lover's smile
contemplating a secret that does not accommodate
his love. It is hatching its own code. Its unavoidable error.

Just the tools

He writes a language unknown to him. Looks up each word in the dictionary when he cannot use his hands to show what he means. He can lick the surface of her skin, taste its tingle and wonders what good words would make of such admission. It is possible to desire. He does not wish for the good. In the end his words are more or less. In my heart, he says, are many rivers. They all flow in the same direction. He sits at a desk every night, in case he is needed. This is his job. He is still waiting to become happy—night after night— watching TV, counting the seconds before actors open their mouths to speak a language he is learning. He repeats after them. Once after a cup of chocolate, he pushes his tongue against hers to show he is the greatest. He counts the seconds. Imagines everybody climbing the stairs into their rooms to hide a secret.

Increments

I am inclined to regret the morning's impossible tasks
supine before me like an impatient lover. Oh, cuttlefish,
I say, but the invocation is a test to see the effectiveness of the
word against a mundane moment. Your garden is allowed no
flowers to bloom in red. Your mother will not grow wise.
Here is a little dog who is loved for her impudence and her
questionable blood. I have not understood you. In the old
books the master has four eyes for four directions. Your
twenty palms are full. You should know this is not the way
to learn. Weeds learn new tricks. They have ingenuity greater
than our needs and wrest all green shoots to wrangle out of
flower pots. They rise in cloaks of sticky and wet tentacles.
Slithering out of their boots to summon all buzzing beings to
their heart. Your window is clear. Your skin has lost its skin.

Two years of winter

Two winters went by without word from him. The elders
stopped calling him by name. Summer came and brought
diseases to plains far from us. Visitors in and out of our house,
left for such places, always too far for mother. Always so
foreign to her even though we lived in the same country.
She spoke no language but one. Called people from the plains,
them, she said they were brought up on different air. She was
not being difficult. Having married one she was in a position
to judge. She said pirates were not efficient on land. Water
allowed for an imaginary sinking not permitted by land.
We were always talking about oceans, tributaries and beaches.
We had pictures of water. We had daytime and nighttime
dreams. To go to the ocean, she said, would be to abandon
reason. In our secret hearts, he was as far from us as he could
be, because he wanted to be found. We would seek him out,
crossing the ocean in our rubber boots, pushing waves with
our bamboo arms. Tethered to the buoys. Stealing his air.

Game

After she left, he did not eat vegetables for a month
but kept to his chair in front of the window, saying
surely, she wasn't serious. How could she? Silly thing,
just like a woman to make decisions on a whim.
Maybe she went to the neighbour's and got trapped
into watching the show about cobras and their memory.
Maybe she's gone walking. Ought he to call the police?
Or was it the family elder? He has walked his nine hundred
steps for the day for the fourth time. He cannot find
his pea-green pullover. He does not know how to make
babies smile. It is summer in the house,
but he is not sure if this is normal. They had names
for every item in their house. A chair was not a chair, no.
It's arms stretched out; it had fangs, it had
a stomach. Its back was straight. It was a game they played.
He tries it now. Says dead, says Gno. Says no. Gno.

Things to remember

The elders of my youth are old and send news of their ailments
precise as recipes they have dealt with. Swollen joints, altered
hairline. Precarious colon. Tartar or torrid nerves?
What does grief provide to functions of a routine? To have lived
another day they say is success. What can I bring them?
No sewing skills, no ditties in dialect, no miracle called Honey
or Sugar. Thirty-three years of seeing the world function still
depends on dialing a three-digit number, and asking a stranger
for help. *What is your name? What are you suffering from?*
The elders want oil rubbed onto their joints, and a lama should
their eyes collapse. They want to know what good all the years
in school did. When did fruits become hybrid? A figure comes
to mind. A reptile is an amphibian. A taste of zucchini. What
does your name mean?

On 21st street

He waits by the window to witness
a disaster. Counts time by the glitter
of a ring, broken glass or hair. The street
emerges—cleaner, glamorous—a rhythm of images
in metallic revolutions. The street, a bridegroom
pinning weight on one single woman thinking alas,
thinking escape. The center of a journey,
a bouleversement when all he wants to do
is sit all day and deliquesce, drop by drop.
He wonders at the octopus who can get
her own drink; at the monkey who entertains
the crowd; the boy or girl called Teddi who
reads backwards from a moving car.
Just for a moment he wants to be a hog
or hot air balloon, deft and droll. He stretches
palms out, traces the lines with a pen. Writes into.

Silver

for Valerie Melvin

She is a chicken with the sky
falling on her. Everyday I wait
for news of forests and four footed
armies capitulating to human
hours. She would like ten arms
of a goddess. Or a thousand
on days when the goldfish
is telling her, not broccoli today,
not tap water. And all ten dogs
on her way to work complain
of hairy legs and ketchup falling
—drying—undiscovered for weeks.
Alpine moon or pink tasseled
porcupines can exist. Ecru is a colour,
she can explain. She knows buildings
are becoming careless as candy
wrappers. Her hand sifts shards
from sand. When I walk,
she has been there.

Lullaby
for Luka, Saamiya and Zenden

We're thinking of you as we do when we offer
to marinate our favorite meat. To charm a star
we'd have to resort to trickery so we'll try
tupperware for toys. The branches of the elm
will carry you only to cities where rivers
of milk flow all seasons. This is the first
fabrication, and an appeasement.
Are you dreaming your mother's dream?
In the ancient texts a child is born to carry
the world forward. In the ancient world
of your mother, farmers sing to the gods
for rain and sing to their mother for wisdom.
In the future already prepared for you,
you will point to us and give us a name.
We will watch your lips form words like petals
and gather them as weapons against the darkness
that comes easily to us. You will provide the
provenance we've been waiting to discover.
You will show us what *this* could mean.

Mother will not grow old

Last night, in a corner of this dark room, I thought of you.
What would you think of the flowers before my window?
Are they of deceptive origin? Do their colours indicate
right motive? Ought I to ascribe to the moon, to the lines
in my palm? Or am I once again asking the wrong questions?
Years go by. I have lived without your help, but you tell me,
when will this end? Words break off from their source except
in dreams where you stand, closer than the stranger I see
on the street. *Mother* is not a word I use anymore.
It serves its purpose well as example and evaluation.
Rapscallion, you. I am aging, I am aging, while you're still
wearing that seaweed green dress we took to the tailor
during her lunch, and she kept a little space in the waist,
just in case, you know. I do not miss you. I do not look
around me seeing mug, slipper, sink, on mornings when the
ordinary is just as it is. But you are here and you're never
going to grow old.

To my friend who works

Our mothers knew better than to wash
clothes when rain was imminent.
They'd encase us in sweaters cocking
our frames upright. How we yearned to walk
and talk at the same time, without popping buttons
or turning woolly knots into tassels hanging from
our frames like we were unknown to ourselves.
We did not want to be elegant poodles strutting
to keep tiny stitches together. We had time, we wanted
to negotiate with the keepers of the forest, the kings
of corner streets with their sticky candies buzzed
and barked at all dusty day. We knew what we wanted,
not this work that kept the elders deaf to the cry
of the ice cream man, the comic man, and the man
dragging the monkey chained to a rope. We knew
what to expect. Our mothers knew. Could tell dust
from debris. Time from age. They shooed us away
from their conversations. Gave us bits of what lay
around them—a lid of a bottle, an empty
match box—that sired children and empires, spitting
and flying. Without wings, without feet.

Surrender

Between the three of us we had a garden of camellias.
The whites were planted in the middle. By the time
we changed our minds, the plants had taken root
and we took it as another lesson. The doctor
often found something wrong in one of us,
we assumed we'd grow feeble before old.
Raindrops left puddles on our clothes laid out,
flattening the grass into our shapes. They would dry
but, again, there was nothing we took for granted.
If the sun came out, if thieves climbed our gates,
if naked spirits tucked damp shirts into their porous
ribs. On our side of the town, we referred to fluctuations
in our collective karma for predictions for weather
and for genes. We had many ways to introduce ourselves
but we said nothing. Said—where are you going?
and, have you eaten today?

Formal links

After this regret of not knowing your name,
one must hope miracles are not called miracles
for a reason. I could begin this as an apology
but I am rarely sorry. I know rumours caught
by newspapers; someone is always at fault.
In this my perfect world, a scabiosa will replace
the rose. The car with six apsos, each with
a hat on her head will not cause an uproar at the
family meeting. My head, she is happy, you say,
but she is alone in it. Everyday you forget,
you may not live forever. You look for the
window where Josephine lives, the curtains
are drawn, the car parked out; things are
as they should be. She will be sitting by
the window seeing the world from her height.
The trees she must not climb, the street she
cannot enter. Her nine lives are guarded.
She will live long through it all.

Lexicon of A.

A home is not a zoo. This refers to the time
when you peeped through bars to look at the lion
brought from another place. A window logic: first
the thin mesh to keep mosquitoes out, then bars
to disparage those given to stealing. Curtains. A little
gap so you can sense movements, register rain, and hide
when jackals come to the door. There are not
many strangers in your town but still mother says
one rotten apple can ruin the basket. Flowers arrest
the forlorn but abiding stare of the dragons on
the wall. A little boy taps at a car hood, tree, wall
as he walks by. He touches the iron gate and the ends
of the jasmine plant twirling at the edges as though
preparing to fly. He calls out: car, leaf, stone, gate,
flower. He says pumpkin patch, pumpkin patch.
It's a secret. It's an effort to name.

Lexicon of age

Summer again. There should be no surprises after
having lived this long. Still, all confirmation of life
remains outside. A silver fish wanders under the desk,
I don't stop to wonder if it will live beyond the day.
Too much water in a person has led to death.
There are exceptions. Water, beyond these hills
of concrete. Across sits a mother with a new son
in her arms. She has not predicted this love.
Pockets bereft of practical jokes. They carry nothing
of use even to sprouting dandelions. Anemia has taken many
of our strong women. *What's up? What's up?*
No sadness in practical tasks. Paper as anchor.
Replies to be made to people unknown.

What's here

That pain is measurable is fanciful; the fact is, it is the heart
that hurts. He looks into the face of deities for sense and
interprets reminders of suffering. Traces of his efficiency
surround him. He wants to give a reason: he has never seen
her handwriting, he doesn't have her mailing address, she
does not know her math. When all is taken into account,
he allows himself a sauna and a cupcake. He writes a story
and it sounds perfect on paper. He keeps his eyes to the East,
where minarets smudge the night like eye shadow. Once
upon a time, he writes, the sky was grunting like an aging
donkey. Once upon a time words were stolen from a nurse's
chart. Aortic chaos. His riven chest.

Salvage

The distance of one word is a quietus but there's
what's left: retrieval or remorse? A mother
lifts her palm to wave as the street whirls around
her; an error of light on her as she stands
in the middle of such bodies. What can she say
to herself when her palms are her own or tucked
into barley. The job has been done. To move
farther and farther away—to say—goodbye.
To indicate a hug. To *see you again*, with a nod
of head. This is the last time. Let's go back
to the interior. The timer. The oven. The blender
and the pestle. These we can explain and understand.
We can start and stop. I do not have the language to pull you
back. To say there she is on her own and she doesn't have
her walking shoes on. To say she was the most
I had. Once she was enough for everything.

Autonomy of the mind

In my family, decisions are made by the lama
who dreams into fate. The gardener who is rotten
whey is not as lucrative as the gardener whose garden
grows tomatoes. After all, we're living through
a conjecture. Wiser to say sorry within the alternatives
of a moment and read the display of toes as assent.
Men are men because we know. The men in my family
hope to return to a country they left in their youth.
They say home and point away from the cement rooms
they have built. At home they say the grass was tall,
the milk was sweet. At home, there was no need for sugar.

Legions under the deceit of summer happily
doff colours unpurposeful as dandruff.
The district you like will have many flowers.
The bridge of your childhood will fall into the river.
Such things happen. We've made time into a chronology,
usurping someone else's bed. What must we fight for?
The sum of a person's life is a precarious calculation
for the rat in the research room. We court our shackles.
We sharpen our tongues. The seven bowls
in our shrine are full of water. We're wearing skin
of ignorance and eyes that will not forget.

The youngest in the family died during the year of his obstacle. A pilgrimage to four holy sites and seven offerings to lamas proved otiose but Doma, the family dog, survived a fall from a steeple. Once a year, the girls on our street worship their brothers with offerings of flowers and vermillion powder, remembering that brothers will one day take wives. We wish to know the ordeals of all beings we pray for. Amphibians. Crocodiles. What of oranges hanging like bats, their discomfort in being ripe? What perpendicular roots we've formed, in this, our neighbhour's motherland. The departed will return but that is not necessarily good.
To be born a human is a commendable feat, the elders say, marking our foreheads with black soot to keep evil eyes away.

She was so wafer-like. I may still love you, she said.
The colour of the morning was the blush of old dirt
and we were not done with the best part of the year.
We took our feet to the river's mouth and hid them there.
I have a chart on my wall, each day I count the days.
There are not enough gods in this new land. The next
day she was crossing the street with a large mangy dog
and everyone stared at her. We pretended not to know
her even though she was our blood. For you my years,
mother said to her. I ask for the sun, in toto. What I tell
you of mother is half of what she was. Think, if words
are rationed, what expressions your face would carry.

To repine reasonably one must have a sense of humor.
The function of the earth is to be constant and to enfold.
This we understand when we learn to walk. In the mountains
there are stories of men who stroll in air, the same men
also draw water out of rocks. You can call us creative;
we entreat our deities for rain and seek the almanac
before we listen to announcements made by the king
in transition. Let's keep the ceremony of little ones
this month; the ritual for the dog, the ritual for money.
Who will supplicate before the male deities in bronze
and in whose language? What will we say when it's all over?

If we are to learn well we must have faith like our mothers
who pray for the happiness of a world they have never seen.
A villain is the man in the film whose intention is to harm
and kill and is resurrected in the next show. A pillory exists
for him as the rehearsal of one more apology is staged
but the logic is often faulty. The death of family members is
not uncommon in my mother's family but most of them
were killed. Still, it's karma so there is no reproach. We pray
for what we are to eat in our mother tongue. We walk
around relics. In this life of our lifetimes, we learn
not to use a headache on an ordinary day to postpone
judgement but we are not to judge. Our mothers say
life is simple because they've learned to ignore it.

A geography of belonging

No river sprung from your head. No enemies turned
to stone as they did in the books. Your hair follicles
do not grow feet like the multiplying demons
we waited so long to die. Dear mother, you gave us
jaggery on the days when the borders were closed
and we stood in the street for petrol and for sugar.
White talcum pearls floated from your armpits.
The black strand of hair under the sofa is yours.
A year is such a short ruler. The King is photographed
in a border town shaking hands with farmers.
When they go home they're still hungry.
There are cracks in the walls of the house.
Everything is changing, but the poor remain so.

The last time we spoke, you talked about cockroaches.
How the kitchen was lost to their fecundity. You could
have done them in. Swept into their hovels in one sweep
of a handmade broom but you'd waited for summer.
And summer kept their heirs alive for a later season.
On your way to work you stop at the butcher's, you nod
to the pharmacist who organizes jars of medicine
to sit like miniature soldiers. My walk is mine.
The world runs above or below, and no one stops
to tell me they can read the future in my face.

Adhering to mindfulness we say nothing.
Mother ate meat. Mother watched spiders
encamp in her domain. Nothing is not what
it seems. We take the animal we are to eat
seriously. After all, a death is involved.
The seven days of our week parted from each
other like warring cousins. In the family tree,
the names of women are missing. In the family
tree the low branches served well as clothesline
and weapon. Once a week we question whether our
country will be free. We are not warriors. We know
a working bowel is proof of a healthy life. We know
people who do not speak our dialect are sitting
at a table. With pen and paper they will map our future.

The anticipation of sleep keeps us awake.
In the heart you have spoken for are tests
for spontaneity. If failure is an option,
we mustn't love, must we? Sweet solitude
separates. Give her a flying broom. If she can
say no to yes and yes to no. If she can eat
a whole chocolate pie it would be just that.
But for the existence of hope, that we should
put out wishes and look to them. There was time
and it could: the dimpled waves, the imperfect
dialogues of legs. Examples used to caution
a hungry nation unable to eat.

One must have brocade ready
for the wedding day. Even if.
Age is no consolation once it is
established. The men who were
not from the right floor or family.
The women who came a little too early.
Some people can see but cannot hear
what is good for them, it is said.
Mothers have their list: a good
person does not sell images of
deities. A good person comes
from recognizable stock. Good does
not have an expiration date, they say.

Not any closer to a decision but walking gives a pretext.
I never had good memory but it hasn't served as excuse.
The polite errors, the wrong names called out in a place
built on common duties. Even the sunflower looks weary.
The youngest in the family has learned her first word.
Mother, she says to the milkman who comes to the door.
In a free country, we say, this girl would have a brother
or a sister. In a free country, her father would be her memory.

A disruption in the humdrum
deceives her into thinking what he says
reflects who she is. She is so good
she can feel good. The daily tutorial comes
with a bibliography. Why must we love
to discover the heart beats for more than one?
She's writing a poem so she won't be impetuous.
She must live with caution. Know her enemies
and regard her friends with disciplined devotion.
She follows a guidebook that shows her what
to expect but not what she must do. It is an
effort to reach a goal. She is so good she knows it.

Toy trains took us from our home in the hills
to the plains where we'd find our uncles
running in and out of the rooms of women
they addressed as sister. We could have
learned to sell jokes in the street.
Ten rupees only if you laugh
we could have said. Instead we learned
to oil prayer wheels and avoid the police
who checked our papers to make sure
we were who we were. Our walls were
full of posters of horses and kung fu actors.
Where could we claim our seat in the future?
Mother had her prayers and father
the language of new trades he fell victim to.
Our parents said we were the flock
to watch out for. We would show
them, they said, how it was done.
In technicolor, they said, in case
there was a misunderstanding.

Time, pinker than the dots
on her blue shirt. A name
wasn't decided because
the lama was travelling
in a foreign country. We
were careless with our
affections. Tiny clouds
were stitched on the baby's
cap. Would she need
happiness or money?
Clouds are for the sky,
says the elder. Breasts
are for milk. Would
we have walked across
the mountains if we
listened to our feet?

First came pictures of animals
not found in our zoo.
Then apparatus assembled
for our benefit because
we had no money in the bank.
Even in the old country
grass was boiled for dinner.
We learn from our elders
so when they said we were
poor, we knew our job
as children. The eldest
gave up school so the youngest
could be polished for reward.
How does this translate in
your language? How can
it be that the rich are thin and
the poor are fat where you live
wrote a little boy from far away.

PHOTO: Marilyn Kennell

TSERING WANGMO DHOMPA was raised in India and Nepal. Tsering received her MA from University of Massachussetts and her MFA in Creative Writing from San Francisco State University. Her first book of poems, *Rules of the House*, published by Apogee Press in 2002 was a finalist for the Asian American Literary Awards in 2003. Other publications include two chapbooks, *In Writing the Names* (A.bacus, Potes & Poets Press) and *Recurring Gestures* (Tangram Press).

Tsering works for a San Francisco based non-profit foundation that provides humanitarian aid to people of the Himalayas.